HISTORY OF BRITAIN

GEORGIAN BRITAIN

1714 to 1837

Revised and updated

Andrew Langley

www.heinemann.co.uk/library
Visit our website to find out more information about Heinemann Library books.

To order:
☎ Phone 44 (0) 1865 888112
🖹 Send a fax to 44 (0) 1865 314091
💻 Visit the Heinemann bookshop at www.heinemann.co.uk/library to browse our catalogue and order online.

First published in Great Britain by Heinemann Library, Halley Court, Jordan Hill, Oxford OX2 8EJ, part of Harcourt Education.
Heinemann is a registered trademark of Harcourt Education Ltd.

Editorial: Lionel Bender and Richard Woodham
Design: Ben White and Michelle Lisseter
Picture Research: Jennie Karrach and Mica Brancic
Production: Helen McCreath

Originated by RMW
Printed and bound in China by WKT Company Limited

10 digit ISBN 0 431 10814 5
13 digit ISBN 978 0 431 10814 8
10 09 08 07 06
10 9 8 7 6 5 4 3 2 1

British Library Cataloguing in Publication Data
Langley, Andrew
Georgian Britain – 2nd ed. – (History of Britain)
941'.07
A full catalogue record for this book is available from the British Library.

Acknowledgements
The publishers would like to thank the following for permission to reproduce photographs:
Page 7 (top): Bridgeman Art Library/British Library, London; Page 7 (bottom): Bridgeman Art Library/Guildhall Library, Corporation of London; Pages 8, 9: Peter Newark's Historical Pictures; Page 10: The Mansell Collection; Page 11 (top): Bridgeman Art Library/City of Edinburgh Museums and Art Galleries; Page 11 (bottom): Peter Newark's Historical Pictures; Page 12: e.t. archive; Page 13: Bedfordshire County Council; Pages 14, 15 (bottom): The Mansell Collection; Page 15 (top): AA Photo Library/Andy Tryner; Page 16: Mary Evans Picture Library; Page 17: e.t. archive; Page 18: The Mansell Collection; Page 19: Bridegman Art Library/Private collection; Page 20 (top): e.t. archive; 20 (bottom): The Mansell Collection; Page 21 (left): Mick Sharp; Page 21 (right): The Mansell Collection; Page 22: Peter Newark's Historical Pictures; Pages 24, 25: e.t. archive; Page 26: Bridgeman Art Library/Private collection; Pages 26 (bottom left), 27, 28: The Mansell Collection; Page 29: Bridgeman Art Library/Yale University Art Gallery, New Haven, USA; Page 30 (bottom left): S & O Mathews; Page 30 (top right): Peter Newark's Historical Pictures; Page 32: Peter Newark's Historical Pictures; Page 33: e.t. archive; Page 34 (top): National Portrait Gallery; Page 34 (bottom): Bridgeman Art Library/National Gallery, London; Page 35 (left): Bridgeman Art Library/Derby Museum & Art Gallery; Page 35 (right): Mary Evans Picture Library; Page 36: e.t. archive; Pages 38–39: Bridgeman Art Library/Christie's, London; Page 39 (top): Bridgeman Art Library/Private collection; Page 40: e.t. archive; Page 41 (top): Bridgeman At Library/British Library, London; 41 (bottom): e.t. archive; Page 42: e.t. archive; Page 43 (top and bottom): The Mansell Collection.

Illustrations by: John James: 6/7, 8/9, 30/31, 32/33, 34/35, 42/43; James Field: 10/11, 12/13, 16/17, 22/23, 26/27, 28/29, 38/39, 40/41; Mark Bergin 14/15, 18/19, 24/25, 36/37.

Cover photograph of Lord Nelson by Sir William Beechey (1753–1839), reproduced with permission of Bridgeman.

Every effort has been made to contact copyright holders of any material reproduced in this book. Any omissions will be rectified in subsequent printings if notice is given to the publishers.

The paper used to print this book comes from sustainable resources.

CONTENTS

*Unfamiliar words are explained in the **glossary** on page 46*

ABOUT THIS BOOK

This book considers the Georgians and the period up to Queen Victoria chronologically, meaning that events are described in the order in which they happened, from 1714 to 1837. Some of the double-page articles deal with a particular part of Georgian history. Those that deal with aspects of everyday life, such as trade, houses, and clothing, are more general and cover the whole period. Unfamiliar words are explained in the glossary on page 46.

▼ **This map** shows the location of places mentioned in the text. The places on the map include large towns, small towns, sites of famous battles, and places of interest.

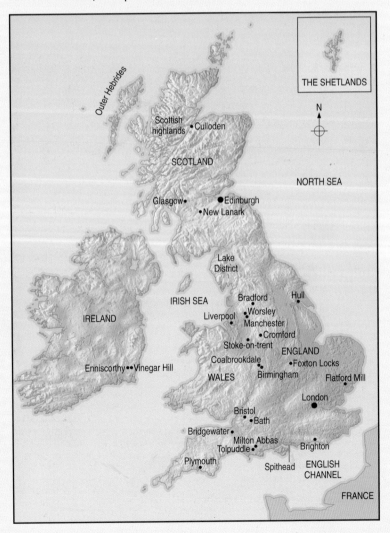

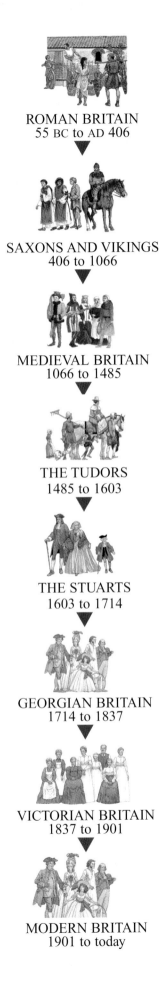

ROMAN BRITAIN
55 BC to AD 406

SAXONS AND VIKINGS
406 to 1066

MEDIEVAL BRITAIN
1066 to 1485

THE TUDORS
1485 to 1603

THE STUARTS
1603 to 1714

GEORGIAN BRITAIN
1714 to 1837

VICTORIAN BRITAIN
1837 to 1901

MODERN BRITAIN
1901 to today

INTRODUCTION

The last Stuart monarch, Queen Anne, died in 1714. All her children had died before she did. So who would rule Britain? The obvious choice was Anne's half-brother, James. But he followed the Roman Catholic religion, and Parliament would not allow a Catholic to become king. (Anne, and Mary II and William III before her, were Protestants.) Instead, the crown was offered to George of Hanover. Although he was a German, George was Protestant and the great-grandson of King James I. He was crowned in October 1714.

This began what we call the Georgian Age. Four kings named George reigned until 1830, followed by William IV until 1837. During much of this time, Britain was at war with France. The two countries struggled for control not only in Europe, but also in North America, the West Indies, and India. Britain was usually the winner, because she had a powerful, well-organized, and skilled navy.

By the end of the 18th century, the British ruled a huge and strong empire. Britain itself had a huge supply of cheap raw materials, such as cotton and sugar, from its colonies. Machines were invented to turn these materials into finished goods more quickly. British traders grew rich selling the goods all over the world. At the same time, better farming methods were used to produce more food to feed the growing population.

All this brought a startling change to the British landscape. The old open fields were enclosed with walls and hedges. Coal mines, iron foundries, and canals were cut into the countryside. New roads were built and new towns began to grow up as people came to find work in the factories.

THE BRITAIN OF WALPOLE

"George I (reigned 1714-27) knew nothing and desired to know nothing; did nothing and desired to do nothing." The author Samuel Johnson said this in 1775. The king left the work of governing the country to his council of ministers. Robert Walpole was to become the most powerful of these ministers.

By 1720, the government was in trouble. The country owed a debt (the national debt) of £54,000,000. Many important people, including politicians and the Royal Family, had also invested money in the South Sea Company. When the company collapsed, Walpole was able to save most of them from disgrace.

After this, Walpole was made First Lord of the Treasury and Chancellor of the Exchequer. He was now the first Prime Minister in British history. Walpole stayed in charge until 1742. He kept his strong position by bribing people to support him.

Walpole tried to make Britain richer. He started a fund to pay off the national debt, and reduced many taxes. Extra money was raised from new import taxes, on tea, coffee, and other goods. He saved money by cutting the size of the army.

▷ **A busy street in early Georgian London.** Walkers, riders and carters jostle with each other. Can you spot these people:
- a beggar?
- a girl selling flowers?
- a street fiddler?
- a fruitseller?
- a gentleman?
- a pedlar?
- coachmen?
- merchants and maids?

Many town streets were narrow, and few were properly paved. In wet weather, they quickly became muddy and rutted. There was a channel down the centre of the street. This was the only drain. People threw out their dirty water from their houses into the street.

Rich and poor. In the early 1700s, rich people lived in large houses in the town centres. But as town centres got dirtier and more crowded, they moved to the outskirts. The old houses were rented out as rooms to poor people. No-one bothered to repair the houses, and many became unsafe and collapsed.

◁ **Sir Robert Walpole** speaks to his council of ministers. Walpole was a very powerful MP, clever, hard-working and an able administrator. He became the first Prime Minister in 1721. Walpole's aims were simple. He wanted to keep taxes low and keep Britain out of foreign wars. He belonged to the Whig group in Parliament, which was opposed by the Tory Party. Walpole was Prime Minister until 1742.

Britain began to grow more prosperous. At this time, most people still lived in villages and small towns. But these were growing and business was expanding. Pedlars carried goods to sell all over the country. Farmers took their animals to market. Others went to the towns to find jobs as servants or street traders. These were better paid than farm work.

The cities grew fast. The population of London rose to more than half a million. Other places, such as Plymouth, Bristol, Manchester, and Glasgow, became big towns, with up to 50,000 inhabitants.

◁ **In 1720, the South Sea Company,** set up to trade with South America under a treaty with Spain, collapsed. Many people who had invested their money in the company in the hope of becoming rich, lost everything. The South Sea 'bubble' had burst, as recorded here.

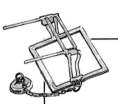

CRIME AND PUNISHMENT

Early Georgian Britain was a violent place. Thieves and muggers roamed the city streets. Highwaymen robbed travellers on lonely country roads. There were frequent riots by mobs protesting against taxes, low wages, or high prices.

Some people stole because they were poor and hungry. Villagers hunted the wild animals (game) on the estates of landowners to feed their families. This was called poaching. Children stole fruit and bread from market stalls because they were starving. But many criminals were brutal and greedy. One of the most famous was Jonathan Wild. He made a fortune by selling stolen goods back to their owners. Wild was hanged in 1725.

Most criminals were never caught. The only law officers were the parish (local area) constables and night watchmen. It was not until 1750 that two London magistrates, John and Henry Fielding, formed a group of men known as the Bow Street Runners. They hunted murderers and thieves. Many of the Runners had once been criminals but had changed sides.

▷ **Gamekeepers seize a poacher,** who is caught in a mantrap. The jaws of this metal trap, hidden in the undergrowth, have snapped shut on his leg. Cruel devices like this were used on many large estates. They were meant to catch poachers or frighten them. There were often battles between keepers and gangs of poachers in which many were injured or killed.

▽ **Dick Turpin,** a famous highwayman of the 1730s and 1740s, escapes his pursuers.

▷ **"Blackbeard" was the nickname** of the savage pirate Edward Teach. He tied burning pieces of rope to his hair to look more terrifying. Blackbeard and his men attacked cargo ships off the American coast. He was killed in 1718. By the late 1720s, the Royal Navy had got rid of most pirates in the Atlantic.

▷ **A pirate is about to be hanged** on gallows beside the River Thames. Huge crowds came to watch such punishments. Some parents even brought their children to watch.

◁ **Smugglers land barrels of brandy** on the coast at night. There was a heavy tax on brandy, an alcoholic drink, and on other foreign goods such as tea. Smugglers avoided paying the tax by secretly bringing in these goods from France and hiding them from tax inspectors. They sold the goods in the towns.

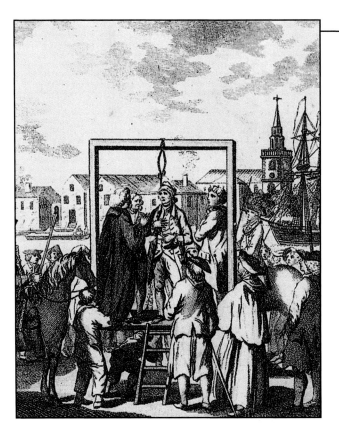

The government tried to keep order with harsh punishments, especially for crimes against people's property. Small crimes were punished by whipping or branding with red-hot irons. Some criminals were tied to the pillory. This was a post in a public place such as a town square. Here, people would throw rotten food and even stones at them.

The worst punishment for crime was hanging. People could be hanged for nearly 200 different crimes. Most of these seem very minor today. Pickpockets and burglars might be hanged next to murderers. In 1723, a new law made poaching a hanging offence.

Although many criminals were never caught, large numbers were executed. During 1750, more than 50 people were hanged in London alone. These included young children. Others were luckier. Their lives were spared and they were transported to work in convict camps in North America.

SCOTLAND AND IRELAND

Many people in Scotland still wanted a Stuart king on the British throne. Their hopes lay at first with the son of King James II, who had been forced from the throne in 1688. The son's name was also James. His supporters were called Jacobites. In 1715, a Jacobite rebellion was easily put down, and James fled to France.

▷ **Jacobite troops (on the left) charge at the Battle of Culloden.** There were only 2,000 of them. They faced an army of 18,000 English, Dutch and Hanoverian soldiers, led by the Duke of Cumberland. Within 40 minutes the rebels were driven back. 'Butcher' Cumberland let his army slaughter over 1,200 of the wounded and captured Jacobites.

△ **Charles Stuart,** or Bonnie Prince Charlie. Although he married in 1772, he had no children. He was the last of the Stuarts to fight for the British throne.

A greater threat appeared in 1745. This was an invasion led by James's son, Charles. He was young, brave and handsome, and was known as Bonnie Prince Charlie. With help from the French, he landed on the Outer Hebrides. Then he sailed to the Scottish mainland and marched southwards with a growing army of men from the Highland clans. They captured Edinburgh and crossed the border into England. But few English people joined the Jacobites. George II sent a large army to oppose them. Charles retreated to Scotland. In April 1746 he met the king's troops at Culloden. Here the rebels were cut to pieces. Charles, like his father, escaped to France.

The British government passed laws to stop any more Jacobite risings. These laws tried to destroy the clan system of the Scottish Highlands. Money and land belonging to rebel leaders were seized by the government.

△ **A view of the High Street in Edinburgh in 1793.** With many new buildings, the city grew into one of the finest in Europe. It also became an important centre for the arts and sciences.

◁ **The Union Jack,** the British flag, was first used in 1801 following the Act of Union between Britain and Ireland. The flag includes the crosses of England, Ireland, Scotland, and Wales.

△ **Cartoon of rebel United Irishmen** practising for their uprising against the British in June 1798. The rebellion was led by Wolfe Tone, and supported by France. It was unsuccessful. Tone attempted to unite Catholics and Protestants to make Ireland independent of Britain. In November 1798 he tried to start another uprising, but was arrested and later committed suicide.

Unrest was growing in Ireland too. Many Protestants had been helped to move there from England during Stuart times to keep the country loyal to Britain. They now owned nearly all the land. Yet two million out of Ireland's three million people were Catholics. Catholics were not allowed to vote in elections nor have important jobs.

During the 1740s, famine increased the anger of the Catholics. Some formed secret societies, which burned houses and attacked Protestants. In 1800, after an unsuccessful rebellion by liberal Protestants, the British government of William Pitt (the Younger) passed the Act of Union. This made Ireland part of the United Kingdom.

FARMING AND FOOD

Farming was still the most important industry in Britain. Most people worked on the land. Farms grew food not only for people, but also for the huge numbers of horses used all over the country. They also produced straw (for thatching), leather, flax (to make clothes), and tallow (an animal fat for candles).

During the 18th century, farming methods began to change and become more efficient. Farmers found new ways of making their land produce more food. They added a kind of clay called marl to help thin soils hold more water. They grew clover and grass-like plants which made the soil more fertile.

▷ **Farm workers enclose a field.** Three of them are planting a hawthorn hedge, while a fourth puts up a gate. Behind them are fields already fenced off. Enclosures provided work for many people. But the new system brought hardship for others. Squatters on common land were forced out. Poor villagers had nowhere to graze their animals or gather firewood so abandoned their homes, as here.

△ **Patriot**, a shorthorn bull, in a painting of 1809. Farm animals grew much bigger and healthier as a result of the work of breeders such as Robert Bakewell. He bred livestock only from his finest animals.

A new system of rotating crops was copied from the Dutch. In each field, the farmer grew wheat one year, turnips the next, then barley, and finally clover. This 'four-course rotation' meant that crops could be grown all the time and the soil was kept fertile. It also provided food to keep animals through the winter, when there was no grass for them to eat. In the past, many had to be killed in the autumn and their meat preserved by salting or smoking. But now cattle, pigs and sheep could be fattened on the extra grain or turnips. Their dung was put on the fields to make the soil more fertile.

▽ **County surveyors** measure land in Bedfordshire before it is enclosed. Each enclosure had to be approved by an Act of Parliament. Between 1750 and 1850, over 2,500 such Acts were passed, and nearly all the open fields in the country were fenced in.

△ **A windmill** drains water from the fens (marshes) in Lincolnshire to use the land for farming.

△ **Turnips** are fed to hungry cattle, which are being kept in a sheltered yard through the winter.

At the same time, the old system of open field farming began to disappear. For many centuries, villages had been surrounded by open fields. Villagers had rented strips of land to grow their crops, and had kept their pigs and geese all together on common land.

Landowners had been gradually enclosing, or fencing in, open land with hedges and walls for many years. But after about 1760, more and more land was enclosed. With fields that were fenced, weeds and diseases did not spread so quickly, and animals could not wander in and trample the crops.

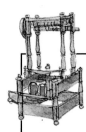

THE RISE OF COTTON

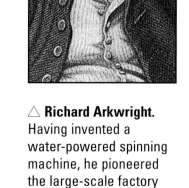

Until the 17th century, most cloth was made from wool. But then a new material became popular – cotton. Cheap cotton cloth was imported from India. The wool manufacturers were alarmed. In 1721, they got Parliament to ban the making of cotton cloth.

△ **Richard Arkwright.** Having invented a water-powered spinning machine, he pioneered the large-scale factory production of cotton yarn.

But people in Britain and Europe wanted cotton. Some cloth manufacturers took no notice of the ban. They imported raw cotton from the West Indies. It was spun into yarn and then woven into cloth. The spinning and weaving was done by outworkers – people who worked at home. As demand grew, new machines made the process faster. The first of these was the flying shuttle, invented by John Kay in the 1730s. The shuttle, which carries thread, could be thrown across the loom.

△ **Houses built for mill workers** in Cromford, Derbyshire. Arkwright opened his first water-powered cotton mill here in 1771.

◁ **Arkwright's Masson Mill** near Cromford as it is today. The water-powered cloth factory was completed in 1784. Attracting workers from all over Derbyshire, it increased Arkwright's employees to more than 5,000. The square tower at the mill (here on the left, in the background) contained a water tank. The round tower was added in 1920 as a flue for steam turbines.

◁ **A mill owner and his wife gaze proudly at their new cotton mill.** It is built in a river valley. The river has been diverted to flow under the mill, where it turns a water wheel. The power from the wheel is passed on by cogs and belts to drive the spinning and weaving machines inside. The new water-powered machines were too big to fit into people's homes. From the 1770s onwards, outworkers had to go to the mills instead.

Kay's invention was being widely used by about 1760. It meant that wider pieces of cloth could be woven more quickly. It also meant that more cotton yarn was needed. Old-fashioned spinning wheels could not keep up with the demand. In 1765, James Hargreaves built a spinning machine called a jenny that allowed not one, but 16, threads to be made at a time.

In 1769, Richard Arkwright invented a water frame for spinning. This was powered by energy from a water mill. In 1785, Edmund Cartwright made the first power looms for weaving. They were driven at first by water, then by steam.

◁ **The spinning jenny,** invented by James Hargreaves in 1765. It could be operated by one person. The frame has 16 rows of spindles. When the worker turns the wheel, the spindles pull and twist the cotton fibres into thread. Later, spinning machines were turned by water power.

STEAM, IRON AND COAL

"I sell here, sir, what all the world desires to have – POWER!" This was how Matthew Boulton described his work to a visitor in 1776. Boulton, and the Scottish engineer James Watt, built steam engines. Steam was rapidly taking the place of old forms of power, such as horses, wind, and water.

Steam engines, using coal-fired boilers, had been built as early as 1698. They were used to pump flood water out of mines. But they could not create a turning force to drive machines. In 1769, Watt made such a steam engine, and it used less coal to heat the water. Soon, engines like this were in use all over Britain. They powered spinning machines and looms in cotton mills. They hoisted coal out of mines. They blew air into furnaces in iron foundries.

Until 1709, iron had been made using charcoal. This was expensive, and it also meant that iron could only be made near forests or other large sources of wood. Abraham Darby began making iron using baked coal, also known as coke. By the 1760s, iron pipes, ploughs and tram rails were being made. The first iron bridge was built across the River Severn in 1779. In 1784, Henry Cort found a way of making iron stronger. The molten metal was stirred so that unwanted material burned away.

As the iron industry grew, so did the demand for coal. In 1700, 2.9 million tonnes of coal were mined. By 1830, the figure had risen to 30 million tonnes. Most of this came from deep mines in north-east England, the West Midlands, and South Wales.

△ **A Watt steam engine of 1788.** The earliest steam engines had simply moved a beam up and down. Watt invented a system of gears and cranks which could turn wheels as well. This made it possible for steam engines to drive machinery. Watt later added a 'governor', a spinning device which controlled the speed of the wheel.

Shown above right is Puffing Billy, a steam locomotive built in 1813. It was used at a colliery to move coal trucks on iron rails.

◁ **An ironworks in the 1780s.** It is built near a coalfield. This provides fuel for the furnaces, which melt and treat the iron ore. Can you spot:
● the water wheel? This powers the bellows which blasts air into the furnace.
● the pumping engines for the mines?
● a giant hammer? Coal is loaded into the furnace. The melted iron from the furnace is cast into bars. A steam engine drives hammers which beat the bars into shape.
● the coal wagons? These are pulled by horses along iron rails. The raised rims on the rails stop the wagons from falling off.
● a horse at work?
● the smoking chimneys?

△ **Two children push a truckload of coal** to the mine shaft. Another child opens the door for them. Many children worked in coal mines. Some 6-year-olds spent all day underground.

LIFE IN THE FACTORIES

As more machines were built, so too were more factories, especially in the north of England. Extra workers were needed to operate the machines. People flocked from the countryside to find jobs in the growing mill towns. Some factory owners even hired children from workhouses.

Factory life was very different from working at home. People worked together in large groups. Boulton's steam engine factory in Birmingham employed over 700 workers. At Josiah Wedgwood's pottery in Staffordshire, there were over 400. Most cotton mills employed about 100 workers.

The machines were all-important. The workers were just "hands" to operate them. But the machines rarely stopped, and always went at the same speed. It was difficult for the workers to keep up with them. Work began at 6:00 a.m. or 7:00 a.m. and went on until 8:00 p.m. Workers had a short break each day for breakfast, and one hour at lunchtime. Sunday was the only day off and the workers were given very few holidays.

▷ **A cotton mill in the 1790s.** The air is full of cotton dust and the noisy roar and rattle of the belts and spindles. It is also very hot and damp, to stop the threads from snapping. The mill owner (in the top hat) inspects some bundles of new cloth. None of the machines has guards or emergency brakes. Many factory workers were injured or killed after getting trapped in the machines. They were not paid if they missed work.

△ **John Wesley** rode all over England holding religious services. In factory towns, many people had lost interest in or had little free time for more organized religion.

▽ **A busy scene at the Corn Exchange** in Mark Lane, London, as illustrated in 1808. Merchants gather to buy and sell corn. It was in places like this that the prices of goods were fixed by traders. There were exchanges in many of the growing industrial towns, such as Manchester, Bradford, and Birmingham.

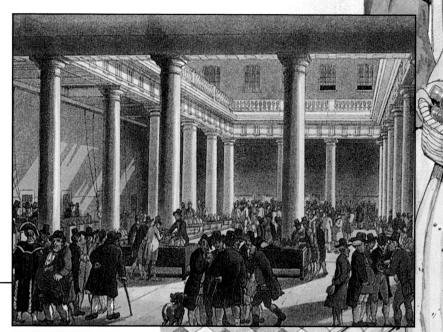

△ **A coloured vase,** which was made in Josiah Wedgwood's pottery at Stoke-on-Trent in about 1780. He also made cheaper pottery that ordinary people could afford to buy.

△ **A girl turns the flywheel** which spins the potter's wheel. In Wedgwood's pottery, child workers were well treated. Wedgwood also encouraged the building of roads and canals.

Mill owners liked to employ women and children, because they could pay them lower wages than men. In Manchester in the early 1800s, nearly half the mill workers were children. Their parents had to send them to work to earn an extra wage. In some families, the children were the only ones who could get work.

Children were given many of the most dangerous jobs to do. Because they were small, they were chosen to crawl under the machines to clear rubbish or blockages. They had to wind the thread on to the spindles and sometimes mend the machines if they broke down.

A few mill owners organized schools for the child workers, and fed them well. But most employers were neglectful or cruel. Children who were lazy, slow at work, or who fell asleep in the factory, would be beaten with a stick or thrown to the floor.

ROADS AND CANALS

At the start of the Georgian age, most roads were in a shocking state. They were muddy and full of deep ruts and potholes. The only good roads were the old Roman ones or turnpikes. Turnpike trusts looked after roads under their control. They made travellers pay a toll for using their roads.

Turnpikes were hated by drovers and poor people, who did not like paying the tolls. But merchants and manufacturers, who could send their goods much more quickly on good roads, liked them. The system grew rapidly. In 1750, there were 5,400 kilometres of turnpikes. By 1830, there were over 32,000 kilometres.

The new roads were stronger and drier. Men such as Thomas Telford and John Macadam developed better methods of road-building. Macadam used a thick layer of small stones which were pressed together by the weight of traffic on top. On these roads, journeys by coach became much faster. But road wagons could not cope with the heavy loads of coal, iron, and other materials needed by industry. Transport by river, canal, and later by rail, was used for these.

▷ **A canal lock,** used to lift boats up and down hills. The lock was a chamber with gates at each end. A boat going uphill pulled by horses entered at the bottom. The gates were closed, and the lock was filled with water, lifting the boat to the upper level. The upper gate was opened and the boat moved out.

▽ **A stage coach timetable** of 1835.

ROYAL MAILS
AND
FAST POST COACHES,
FROM THE
Swan Hotel, Birmingham.

	MORNING.	EVENING.
LONDON TALLY-HO! thro' Coventry in 11 hours	8	
LONDON—Day, thro' Oxford	¼ past 10	6
LONDON—Royal Mail		7
LONDON—Greyhound	½ before 5	
LONDON—Express		7
ALCESTER and REDDITCH		7
BANBURY		9
BATH	½ before 7	
BRISTOL	8 and 9	

▷ **A stage coach is about to pass through a turnpike.** These were the fastest vehicles on the road, travelling at about 19 km/h. They carried passengers and mail bags. The cheapest seats were on top, where there was a risk of cold and wet. Behind the coach rode guards with their guns.

20

◁ **Locks on the canal at Foxton,** Leicestershire. Two groups of five locks were built in 1814. They raised boats 22 metres. The lock keeper lived in a cottage by the canal. He opened and shut the lock for narrow boats travelling. Canal transport was cheap.

△ **Richard Trevithick's early steam locomotive,** called *Catch-me-who-can*, on show in Euston Square in London in 1809.

In 1759 the first British canal was built by James Brindley. It carried coal from the Duke of Bridgewater's mines at Worsley 10 kilometres to the factories and ironworks of Manchester.

In the next 50 years, over 6,000 kilometres of new canals were dug. They formed a network which linked the main industrial towns of England and Wales with London and the sea ports.

BUILDING AN EMPIRE

When George II was told that General James Wolfe was mad, he said "Mad, is he? Then I hope he will bite some of my other generals." Wolfe was one of the brilliant military leaders who won vital battles in the late 1750s. These victories helped Britain to set up an empire in North America and India.

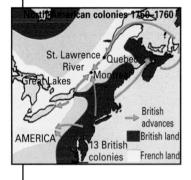

△ **Britain expands its North American territories.**

▷ **A painting of the battle for Quebec in 1759.** Boatloads of British soldiers row up the St Lawrence. Others are climbing up to the flat Plains of Abraham. Here they are formed into ranks to face the French attack. (Below) Wolfe was wounded in the battle and died soon afterwards.

Britain's main rival for overseas trade and colonies was France. The French controlled much of the fur and timber trade in Canada. They had built a chain of forts to stop British settlers getting to the west. The British Secretary of State, William Pitt, was determined to drive the French out of North America.

In 1759, Pitt chose General Wolfe to lead an attack on the French town of Quebec, on top of a steep cliff above the St Lawrence River. Wolfe decided on a bold plan. He landed his troops by night on the river bank. They scrambled up the cliffs and drove back the astonished French soldiers. The British captured Quebec, but Wolfe died in the battle.

The British armies advanced through the Great Lakes. By September 1760 they had captured Montreal and gained control of all Canada. This huge territory was added to the 13 American colonies already ruled by Britain on the east coast.

Meanwhile, Britain and France had also been fighting in India. The merchants of the English East India Company had been trading there since 1600. But by the 1740s France had strong trading bases as well. The French ruled large areas of central and southern India, and were supported by local princes.

One of these princes, Siraj-ud-Daulah, seized the British trading post at Calcutta in 1756. A British force led by Robert Clive set out from Madras. Clive recaptured Calcutta, and went on to defeat Siraj-ud-Daulah at Plassey in June 1757.

This weakened French power in India. By 1761, they had been driven out of Pondicherry, one of their last strongholds. The East India Company took over the running of Bengal, and grew very rich. Gradually British trade and control of the country's wealth increased. By 1814 the Company ran three-quarters of the land for the government.

▷ **In India,** Britain, France, Holland, and Portugal had set up trading posts in the 17th and early 18th centuries. Following Clive's victory at Plassey, the East India Company controlled a population greater than that of Britain at the time.

Indian campaign 1740–1814

Bengal
Plassey
INDIA
Calcutta
☐ Mogul Empire
■ British colonies
Madras
Pondicherry

◁ **Fighting during the Battle of Plassey in 1757.** Clive had 3,200 men, including over 2,000 Indian soldiers. This was a tiny force compared with Siraj-ud-Daulah's army. This consisted of 35,000 infantry and 18,000 cavalry, plus a small number of French soldiers. It also had 50 field guns, which were pushed into place by Indian elephants. However, accurate British shooting soon forced Siraj to retreat.

23

SLAVERY AND TRADE

"The slaves lie in two rows, one above the other, on each side of the ship, close to each other, like books upon a shelf. The poor creatures are bound in chains." This description was written in 1788 by John Newton, who had once been the captain of a slave ship.

Slaves were a vital part of British trade in the Atlantic, as they had been since Stuart times. Ships from Liverpool and Bristol carried cotton cloth and iron goods to West Africa. There, these items were swapped for slaves. The slaves were taken across the Atlantic and sold to work on the sugar plantations in the West Indies. Then, the slave traders loaded the ships with sugar, tobacco, and other raw materials and sailed back to Britain. This three-sided trade made huge profits for the owners of the ships, plantations and cotton factories.

It also caused terrible suffering to the slaves. They were snatched from their villages and packed below decks with no room to move. Many died on the voyage to the West Indies. Life was just as bad on the plantations. Between 1712 and 1768, over 200,000 slaves were taken to Barbados alone. Yet the population of the island only increased by 26,000 in that time. In 1788 a campaign to abolish slavery was begun.

▷ **A group of slaves is forced on board** a British slave ship at a West African port (far right). The Africans have been kidnapped from their home villages by slave traders, roped together, and marched to the coast. Hundreds of slaves were packed into the ships (as shown right). The more that were crammed on board, the more the captain would be paid. In 1771 alone, 50,000 slaves were shipped from Africa.

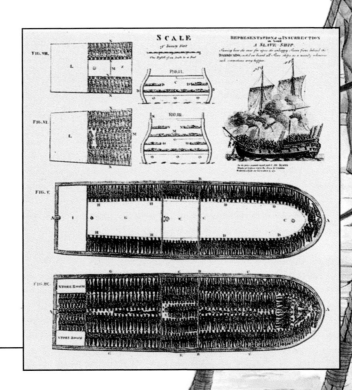

△ **African slaves on board ship** – from a painting of about 1750. The slaves' price in Africa might be £3 each. At an auction in the West Indies their price would be £25.

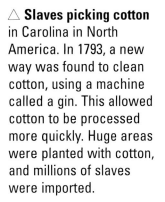

△ **Slaves picking cotton** in Carolina in North America. In 1793, a new way was found to clean cotton, using a machine called a gin. This allowed cotton to be processed more quickly. Huge areas were planted with cotton, and millions of slaves were imported.

△ **The riches of the British Empire.** On the table are:
● tea from India
● sugar from the West Indies
● spices from Sri Lanka
● cotton cloth from North America. The lady wears a dress made from Chinese silk.

During the 18th century, Britain grew into the most powerful trading nation in the world. Exports increased greatly in value.

The secret of this success was Britain's growing empire overseas. All goods from the colonies were shipped to British ports. From India came tea, silk, and spices. From Canada came furs and fish. From the West Indies came sugar, cotton, and tobacco. These goods were processed in British factories. Cotton was woven into cloth, sugar was refined, and tobacco was cured. The finished products were sold at home and overseas.

At first, most exports went to countries in Europe. But by 1800 the biggest buyers of British products were the West Indies and North America.

COOK AND AUSTRALIA

By 1765, Britain controlled vast areas of land in North America and India. But another huge area of the world was still a mystery. This was the southern Pacific Ocean. People believed there was a massive unknown continent there. In 1768 the British government sent a ship, the *Endeavour*, to explore the Pacific region.

The *Endeavour's* captain was James Cook. After exploring the island of Tahiti, Cook sailed on to New Zealand. His men became the first Europeans to land there. Further west, Cook reached Australia. Dutch sailors had been exploring its north and west coasts since the 1600s. They had found only wild land. Cook was the first to find the more fertile and sheltered west coast around Botany Bay. He claimed the region for Britain.

Although Australia was huge, it was not the great unknown continent people were looking for. In 1772, Cook explored much further south. He even crossed the Antarctic Circle. But he never reached the southern continent, Antarctica.

▷ **Captain James Cook,** painted by Nathaniel Dance in about 1766. Cook was an outstanding leader, mapmaker and navigator. In 1759, his charting of the St Lawrence River had helped Wolfe in his attack on Quebec. His three great voyages between 1768 and 1779 explored huge unknown areas of the Pacific Ocean. At the Hawaiian Islands he was tragically killed by the islanders. Cook's signature is shown below.

▽ **Maoris watch as Cook's ship *Endeavour* arrives on the New Zealand coast.** The Maoris were warlike people, and attacked the foreigners when they first tried to land on the islands.

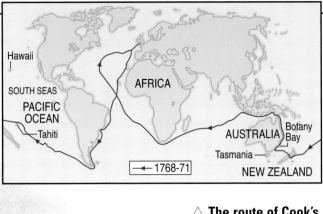

△ **The route of Cook's first voyage.** On the *Endeavour,* he travelled with scientists who brought back to Britain many of the unusual animals they discovered. They were baffled by the fact that animals like the koala lived nowhere else.

△ **Cook's crew** being served fruit and vegetables. The fresh food helped to prevent scurvy, a common disease on ships at the time.

△ **In his second ship,** *Resolution,* Cook finds his way blocked by a range of ice mountains. All around are icebergs and sheets of pack ice.

Cook's discovery of Botany Bay came just in time for the British government. For many years, they had been transporting criminals to the American colonies. But the colonies rebelled against British rule in 1776. Another remote place had to be found for the criminals. In May 1787, 8 years after Cook's death, a fleet of 11 ships sailed from England. They carried 736 criminals, guarded by 200 soldiers. The fleet reached Botany Bay early in 1788. The European settlement of Australia had begun. Many of the prisoners stayed there to live once their sentences were over. During the 1790s, they were joined by ordinary people from Britain.

◁ **Convicts** at Hobart on Van Diemen's Land (Tasmania), being marched to work. Over 130,000 convicts were transported to Australia between 1788 and 1818. Most had to work on the farms of local settlers. The worst criminals were chained together in gangs. They wore yellow prison clothes, and were known by the free settlers as canaries.

THE AMERICAN REVOLUTION

"These United Colonies are, and of right ought to be, free and independent states." This is part of the Declaration of Independence, written in 1776. It was written by Thomas Jefferson and other American leaders, who wanted to be able to govern themselves.

▷ **Colonial rebels** fire at a force of Scottish troops fighting for Britain at the Battle of Moore's Creek Bridge in North Carolina in 1776.

△ **The Boston protest,** or Tea Party, of 1773.

▽ **The 13 American colonies** at the beginning of the War of Independence in 1775.

War of Independence 1775-83

Saratoga (US)
Princeton (US)
Trenton (US)
Yorktown (US)
Norfolk (US)

Lexington
Boston (Brit)
New York (Brit)
Chesapeake Bay (US)

N

● British/US victory

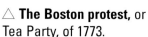

The 13 American colonies had been unhappy with British rule for several years. The British government controlled their trade and made them pay taxes. The colonists had to export most of their goods to Britain.

Then, in 1764, the British started to demand more and more taxes from the colonists. They had to pay duty (extra charges) on sugar, glass, paper, tea, and other imported goods. There were violent protests against the taxes.

Top: British musket   Bottom: American rifle

△ **A British** 'redcoat' soldier in his brightly coloured uniform, and an American militia man (right), harder to spot in his dark clothes. The Redcoat's musket could be loaded quickly, but the American's rifle was more accurate.

The Tea Act of 1773 allowed the East India Company to sell its tea in America at the cheapest price and so boost its income. In Boston, protesters raided British ships and threw the tea overboard.

The British tried to punish the Bostonians for their action. They closed the harbour and stationed troops there. In April 1775, the troops clashed with American soldiers at Lexington. Here, the first shots were fired in the colonies' fight for independence.

The war lasted for 8 years. The British had over 34,000 well-trained troops. But their supplies had to come from Britain. They won some early battles, but could not take control. In 1777, a British army was surrounded at Saratoga and forced to surrender. The French were glad to see their old enemy defeated, and joined the war on the American side. Spain gave its support to the colonists in 1779.

By now it was clear that the British could not win. And George III, ignoring the advice of his ministers, refused to let the colonies have their own way or make a deal. In October 1781, the British surrendered at Yorktown in Virginia.

◁ **American leaders sign the Declaration of Independence in 1776.** The main battles: 1775 Bunker Hill, Boston – the British win, but lose over 1,000 men. 1776 New York – another British victory. Trenton – colonials, led by George Washington, win their first battle.

1777 Princeton – the British are driven back. Saratoga – British surrender; 6,000 become prisoners. 1780 Charleston – falls to the British. 1781 Chesapeake Bay – British fleet badly damaged by the French. Yorktown – final defeat for the British.

HOUSES AND HOMES

As Britain's population increased, many more houses had to be built. And, as some people grew richer, their new houses became grander. This was a great age of building, from the factory towns of the north to the centres of fashion such as Bath and Edinburgh.

Grandest of all were the large country houses of the rich and powerful. These were decorated with pillars, moulded plaster, and huge oil paintings. Their gardens and parks were dotted with lakes, temples, and fountains.

Georgian town houses were usually built in rows. Straight rows were called terraces, and curved rows were called crescents. Some terraces were arranged around an open space in squares. The houses were made of stone or brick. Since the Fire of London in 1666, buildings could not be made of wood.

For the poor, however, housing got little better. Farm labourers lived in two- or three-roomed cottages which were often damp and draughty. Near factories and coal mines, rows of tiny houses were built very cheaply for the workers.

▷ **Servants slept in the attic bedrooms** at the top of the house. Even a modest town house needed several servants to do the daily work. A kitchenmaid helped the cook, while a chambermaid cleaned rooms. Footmen did the heavier jobs and answered the front door.

▽ **The Royal Crescent** in Bath, built by John Wood the Younger in 1767.

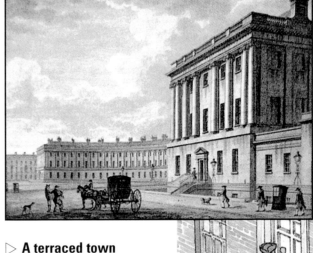

▷ **A terraced town house** belonging to a middle class family in the 1780s. Although its front is narrow, the house is two rooms deep. In the basement are the kitchen and scullery. Above these are the grand reception room and dining room. The first and second floor rooms have tall windows to give plenty of light.

◁ **Thatched cottages** in Milton Abbas, Dorset. The village was created by Lord Milton, Earl of Dorchester, in the 1770s.

▽ **A coach being cleaned in the mews,** a narrow street behind the houses. The household's coaches and horses were kept here. When the family wanted to go out, the coach was driven round to the front door for them to board.

◁ **Architects designed the insides of houses** to look impressive, with decorated walls, fireplaces, and doorways. Furniture included sofas, writing desks, and tables made by famous craftsmen of the time.

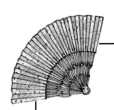

FOOD, DRINK, AND CLOTHING

In Georgian times, Britain was one of the best-fed countries in the world. Food was cheaper than ever before. And as farming methods improved, more meat, grain, milk, and butter were produced. New kinds of food and drink, such as potatoes, sugar, coffee, and tea, came from the colonies overseas.

▷ **A cottager** cooks a meal at the fire. Country people usually baked their own bread and brewed their own beer. But many workers in the towns bought bread and pies from shops or street traders. Rich people bought all their food, and clothes, from shops in towns (far right).

△ *Gin Lane*, a cartoon of 1751 by William Hogarth showing people in London spending their money to get drunk on cheap gin. This was a major cause of poverty and death at the time.

It was not only the rich who ate well. The middle classes, such as lawyers and farmers, usually had huge meals. For breakfast, there were lamb chops, steaks, eggs, cheese, and beer. Lunch was a lighter meal, but dinner was eaten early, at about 5:00 p.m. Dinner consisted of several courses, including fish, beef, pork, duck, salad, and cheese, followed by nuts and oranges.

Mealtimes were much less exciting for the poor. Farm labourers lived mostly on brown bread, potatoes, and bacon. They often had a small patch of ground to grow vegetables or keep a pig on. In Scotland, the main diet was milk and oatmeal porridge, while in Ireland it was milk and potatoes. Workers in the towns could not grow anything, and had to buy most of their food from shops.

Gentleman   Lady   Craftsman

Lady's daughter   Merchant

△ **18th-century clothes and fashions.** The people shown here are wearing typical styles of the day. On the left is a wealthy gentleman and his family. Rich people spent large sums of money on fine clothes.

▷ **This cartoon by famous Georgian artist Thomas Rowlandson** dating from about 1800 makes fun of the huge meals many people ate. (Notice not only the size of the two men seated at the table but also the dishes they are being served.) The English were famous throughout Europe for their greed and fatness. They were especially fond of meat and wine.

Rich people could afford many nice clothes. Men who followed every changing fashion were called dandies. They dressed in tight-fitting trousers or breeches, tail coats, and high collars. Women wore dresses made of heavy silk or muslin. On their heads they wore wigs, which were powdered and curled. Many poor people only had one set of clothes, which were usually made of cotton and that they wore all the time. Many of them could not afford shoes. In winter, they tied straw or sacking round their feet to keep them warm.

Factory owner   Squire   Country lad   Farm worker   Groom

Working class children   Milkmaid   Boy chimney-sweep   Farm boy

Some wealthy men covered their heads with huge curled wigs. Women wore their hair piled high and decorated with jewels. Their servants, such as the coachman and groom, had uniforms to show their importance. But for most poorer people, clothes were little different from Stuart times. Many children, such as the sweep's boy, had only rags to wear. They had to beg, steal, or borrow most of their clothes.

SCIENCE AND THE ARTS

In the 1760s, science became popular. People had fun giving each other electric shocks. Meanwhile, more serious work was being done by scientists such as Joseph Priestley. In 1774, he discovered that air contained the gas oxygen. Later, Henry Cavendish proved that water was made of oxygen and hydrogen.

One of the most famous British scientists of the age was Humphry Davy. In 1799 he found that a gas called nitrous oxide could be used to put patients to sleep before surgery. It is sometimes called laughing gas. Davy went on to discover many new chemicals and to invent a safety lamp for miners.

In medicine, the Scotsman William Smellie developed new methods which made childbirth safer for women. And in 1796 Edward Jenner began vaccinating people with a mild disease called cowpox. This protected them from smallpox, which was much more harmful and often deadly.

◁ **Samuel Johnson.** In 1764 he founded The Literary Club, a group of popular Georgian authors in London.

▷ **Jane Austen** became the most famous authoress of her time.

▷ *Mr and Mrs Andrews,* **a portrait by Thomas Gainsborough.** Gainsborough liked to paint people in a rural, outdoor setting. He was famous for his portraits of rich people. In 1768, he helped to found the Royal Academy of Arts in London, with financial assistance from George III.

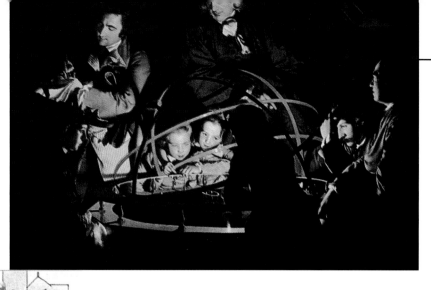

▽ **Musicians play** for royal celebrations in May 1749. The music was written for the king by the German composer George Frederick Handel. Handel had come to live in England in 1712. Here he wrote many famous choral works based on Bible stories, including the *Messiah* in 1742.

△ **Studying a model of the solar system** – a painting of science education at the Royal Institution, which was founded in London in 1799 to promote science.

△ **An illustration from *Frankenstein*,** written by Mary Shelley in 1818. This novel tells the story of a scientist who creates a human from parts of dead bodies.

This was also an exciting period for British literature. In 1755, Samuel Johnson finished his huge English Dictionary, which explained the meanings of more than 40,000 words. At the same time, the first of the great English novels began to appear, such as Henry Fielding's *Tom Jones*.

In the first half of the 18th century, poetry was witty and clever, but written in a strict and artificial way. By the 1780s, poets were using more natural and simple language. Robert Burns, a Scots farmworker, wrote many poems, including *Auld Lang Syne* (The Days of Long Ago), which are still famous all over the world. In 1798, the poets William Wordsworth and Samuel Taylor Coleridge wrote about Nature and fantasy with such deep feeling that these became popular literary subjects. Their ideas were followed by such poets as Percy Shelley and John Keats, who became known as the Romantics.

NELSON'S NAVY

The Royal Navy was Britain's strongest fighting force. It was used to defend the island, to attack other navies, to control distant colonies and to protect merchant ships. Britain's control of the seas made her one of the most powerful nations in the world.

▷ **A sailor in the Royal Navy prays before battle.** He is joking about the dangers ahead and his share of the prize money. A 'prize' was a foreign vessel captured by a British warship. The money for the value of the prize was divided amongst the ship's crew. The officers got the biggest share.

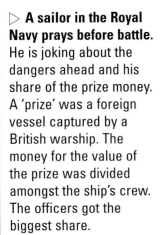

△ **Admiral Horatio Nelson** was the greatest naval commander of the age. His bold leadership brought vital victories against the French fleet. Nelson was killed at the Battle of Trafalgar in 1805.

▽ **A British warship of the 1790s** (shown in cutaway to reveal details below the main deck).

The Navy was able to expand quickly if there was a threat of war. In 1789, there were only 16,000 officers and men. But by 1803, during the war against France, this number had risen to 120,000. Over 110 warships patrolled trade routes and the coasts of Britain's empire.

These ships were made entirely of wood. A big warship, such as Horatio Nelson's flagship *Victory,* might use up the timber from woodland the size of 40 football pitches. It could be armed with up to 110 guns. These fired round shot at an enemy ship, to make holes in the hull or bring down the masts. The aim was to damage the other ship so that it could not sail. The riflemen shot at the enemy officers from the rigging. Finally, marines (navy soldiers) and sailors would board and capture the ship.

A warship had a crew of several hundred men. There had to be plenty of sailors to load and fire the guns, and to alter the sails. Beside these were officers, cooks, carpenters and sailmakers, and the surgeon. About half of the crew were criminals or seamen forced into service by the "press gang".

△ **Members of a ship's crew:** (from left to right) midshipmen, cook, topman, carpenter, cabin boy.

◁ **Different "rates" (sizes) of warships.** First-raters carried over 100 guns. Second-raters carried 84 to 100 guns. Third-raters had 70 to 84 guns. The 27 ships in Nelson's fleet at Trafalgar had more than 2,200 guns between them.

▽ **Life on board ship** was harsh. The food (left) was of poor quality. Wrongdoers were punished with the lash (centre). Many were injured by their own guns (right).

WAR AGAINST NAPOLEON

In 1789, a violent revolution started in France. The French king and his queen were executed, and thousands more died. Out of the chaos rose Napoleon Bonaparte. He took control of the French government in 1799 and began to build up an empire in Europe.

Napoleon was a skilful and ambitious general. In 1802, he signed a peace treaty with Britain, but continued to harm its overseas trade. The government became alarmed at his rising power. In 1803, the French planned to invade Britain. But first they had to dodge the British fleet, led by Lord Nelson. Nelson cornered the enemy warships at Cape Trafalgar near Gibraltar in 1805 and destroyed them. The danger of invasion was over.

Yet Napoleon won victories on land. By 1807, he had gained control of Spain and put his brother on the Spanish throne.

▷ **The Duke of Wellington** led the allies in the victory against Napoleon at the Battle of Waterloo in 1815. He later became Prime Minister. Napoleon Bonaparte built up a massive French Empire in western, southern, and central Europe.

The Duke of Wellington

Napoleon Bonaparte

In 1808, a British army was sent to Spain. It was led by Sir Arthur Wellesley, who later became the Duke of Wellington. During what was called the Peninsular War, he helped the Spanish and Portuguese to drive the French out of the land. After being defeated at Vittoria in 1813, Napoleon's troops fled back to France. Wellington followed them.

Meanwhile, Napoleon himself had tried to invade Russia. This was a disaster, in which the French lost half a million men. During 1814, the allied armies (which included the British) swept into France and captured Paris. Napoleon surrendered. He was sent into exile on the Mediterranean island of Elba. A year later he escaped, only to meet final defeat at Waterloo.

▷ **British infantry at Waterloo** in Belgium. During the battle, the soldiers stood in squares, facing outwards with their muskets and bayonets. These squares stood firm against the attacks by the French cavalry. Late in the day, Prussian troops arrived and helped to smash Napoleon's forces.

▽ **A painting of the Battle of Waterloo.** The Duke of Wellington is urging his infantry forward.

Waterloo forces and casualties. The allied forces consisted of 21,000 British, 22,000 Prussian, and 24,000 Dutch and Belgian soldiers. There were 22,000 allied casualties. The French army contained 71,000 men, and lost 41,000.

◁ **Cartoon showing the defeated Napoleon** being sent in exile by the French to the island of Elba in 1814.

The major battles of the Napoleonic Wars:
1798 The Nile: Nelson defeats the French fleet.
1800 Marengo: Napoleon enters northern Italy.
1805 Trafalgar: Nelson destroys the French fleet.
1805 Austerlitz: Napoleon defeats the Russian and Austrian armies.
1809 Talavera: Wellington defeats French in Spain.
1812 Borodino: Napoleon captures Moscow but his starving army is soon forced to retreat.
1813 Leipzig: An allied army pushes the French out of Germany.
1815 Waterloo: Napoleon's final defeat.

RIOTS AND REBELLION

The Georgian period was a time of great unrest. Riots, marches and protests were common, especially after the 1750s. The rioters were mostly poor people. They were angry for many reasons – low wages, high food prices, turnpike tolls, and enclosures. Now and then, soldiers had to be sent to stop these uprisings.

During the 1790s, this unrest grew worse. There were two main reasons. The first was the French Revolution, which had begun in 1789. It inspired many British people to fight for a fairer system of government, with no monarch as leader. In 1795, a shot was fired at George III, and his coach was pelted with stones. "No war! No famine! No king!" shouted the mob.

The second reason was the increasing use of machines. Spinners and weavers feared that the new spinning jennies and power looms would put them out of work. Gangs of them smashed machines and burned down factories. Meanwhile bad harvests made bread prices higher still. Between 1793 and 1815 there were over 700 major riots. There were even mutinies by seamen of the Royal Navy at Spithead and off the Essex coast.

▽ **Three men run away** after setting fire to a hayrick and smashing a threshing machine during the "Captain Swing" riots of 1830. (Two of the men are badly disguised as women.) The rioters were desperate for food and a living wage. Enclosures made over many years had taken away much of the common land where they used to graze animals and gather firewood.

▷ **A group of trade unionists** from Tolpuddle, Dorset, carry a petition to William IV in 1834 to ask that six villagers should not be transported to Australia. The six Tolpuddle Martyrs were farm workers who had taken an oath of loyalty to a trade union. This was against the law. The petition was not successful and the Martyrs were sentenced to seven years labour in Australia. But in 1836 they were released and sent back to Britain.

There were 316 cases of arson (setting fire to property) between 1830 and 1832. Over 500 people were transported following these outbursts, and 19 were executed.

◁ **In Manchester in 1819,** a peaceful crowd of 80,000 people met in St Peter's Fields to demand political change. They were charged by soldiers waving swords. Eleven of the crowd were killed. The tragedy was called Peterloo in mockery of Waterloo.

The government punished the rebel leaders. In 1799 it passed a new series of laws called the Combination Acts. These banned workers from meeting to form combinations (trade unions). But they did not stop the machine-smashers. A group of these banded together in 1811. They called themselves Luddites, after an imaginary leader, Ned Ludd. The Luddites damaged factories in many parts of the English north and Midlands.

Among the poor in the countryside, wages for farmworkers were very low, and thousands were unable to afford enough food. In 1830, workers in south-east England burned hayricks and attacked farms in protest.

◁ **The Reformers' attack on the Old Rotten Tree** in 1817. The names of "rotten boroughs" are written on nests in the tree. As people moved from rural areas to towns, these boroughs were left with only a few electors but still the same number of MPs as before. By contrast, some towns with growing populations had no MPs, which was unjust.

SOCIAL REFORM 1800–1837

As the 19th century began, so did a series of reforms, or changes. These were the result of determined work by just a few people, who wanted to make life easier for poor people, their children, criminals, and slaves. The reforms were not usually welcomed by the government.

One of the reformers was William Wilberforce. As early as 1785, he began a campaign to end slavery. It was not until 1807 that Parliament stopped the slave trade. But slaves in the British colonies were not set free until 1833.

Some people believed that poor children in factories were treated as slaves. In 1802, mill-owner Robert Owen persuaded Parliament to help them. A new law stopped children from working more than 12 hours a day, or at night. They also had to be given daily lessons.

The hated Combination Acts were repealed (abolished) in 1824. Now workers could meet together and form trade unions. This helped them to seek higher wages. By 1834, there were over 800,000 trade unionists.

The main reforms in the prison system:
1808 Pickpockets to be transported for life, instead of hanged. They were shipped to Australia.
1817 Elizabeth Fry begins her campaign for better conditions in women's prisons.
1821 Farm school opens in London, aimed at educating child prisoners.
1823 Death sentence lifted from 130 minor offences. Prisons, like the prison ship above, to be paid for out of the local taxes. Jailers to be paid wages, instead of fees from prisoners. Prisoners to get better food and health care.

▷ **Robert Owen's factory mills, housing estate, and school** at New Lanark, near Glasgow. Owen was a rich factory owner who treated his workers well. He paid them good wages and built comfortable houses. He refused to employ children younger than 10 years old.

▽ **Elizabeth Fry visits a women's prison** in 1817. At the time, these prisons were often filthy and violent places. Fry's work changed them. She made sure that the prison officers were all women, and that the prisoners had better clothing, beds, and education.

△ **Rich people** visit women in a workhouse. The new Poor Law of 1834 forced the very poor to live in their local workhouse.

△ **Women and children** cleaned factory machines. In 1833 a new law made it illegal for children under the age of 9 to work in cotton mills.

△ **William Wilberforce** began his work to abolish slavery after meeting the captain of a slave ship. By the time he succeeded, he was an old man.

The treatment of criminals also changed. In 1806, Samuel Romilly set out to reduce the number of crimes that could be punished by death. By 1823 (after Romilly's death), the death sentence had been lifted from over 100 offences.

The biggest campaign of all was to reform the voting system. Only the rich and owners of property could vote in elections. After a long struggle, the Great Reform Act was passed in 1832. This gave more people the vote, and let people in the new industrial towns elect MPs.

◁ **Constables in the first police force,** set up in 1829. They were called Peelers or Bobbies after the Home Secretary, Sir Robert Peel. There were 1,000 constables, mostly ex-soldiers, who patrolled the streets of London. They wore uniforms of top hats and dark blue coats, and carried wooden truncheons.

THE POLICE WEAR BEARDS AND MOUSTACHES. PANIC AMONGST THE STREET BOYS.

Famous people of Georgian times

Jane Austen, 1775–1817, wrote six witty novels, in which she made fun of the manners of her time (see page 34). They are still very popular stories, and include *Pride and Prejudice* and *Emma.*

Fanny Burney, 1752–1840, was an English writer. She knew many famous people, and wrote about them in her letters and diaries.

Fanny Burney

John Constable, 1776–1837, was a painter of landscapes. Many of his paintings are of the countryside of the county he lived in, Suffolk.

Henry Fielding, 1707–1754, was a London magistrate and a writer. His comic story *Tom Jones* is one of the earliest great English novels.

David Garrick, 1717–1779, was the most popular actor of the age. He used realistic scenery and made sure that the audiences behaved themselves.

George I, 1660–1727, became king on the death of Queen Anne. He was German and spent most of his reign in Hanover, Germany, never having learned English (see pages 6, 7).

George II, 1683–1760, was the son of King George I. He ruled from 1727. He was the last English king to lead his army in battle (at Dettingen in Germany in 1743) (see pages 10, 22).

George II

George III, 1738–1820, became king in 1760 after his grandfather George II. He was a keen farmer but a poor ruler (see page 29). He also suffered periods of mental illness. After 1811, his son ruled as Prince Regent.

George IV, 1762–1830, was Prince Regent until his father's death in 1820, when he became king. A greedy man, he was an unpopular monarch.

William Herschel, 1738–1822, and his sister **Caroline Herschel,** 1750–1848, were astronomers born in Germany. They settled in England. In 1781, William discovered the planet Uranus. Caroline discovered new comets.

John Keats, 1795–1821, was one of the greatest of the Romantic poets. Among his best-known poems are *Ode to a Nightingale* and *Ode to Autumn.* He died very young of tuberculosis.

Thomas Malthus, 1766–1834, was the first person to study the effects on standards of living of a growing population. He argued that population growth was only held back by war and other disasters.

Daniel O'Connell, 1775–1847, led the campaign for Roman Catholics to become MPs. He also fought for the social and political rights of Irish Catholics.

Thomas Paine, 1737–1809, wrote *The Rights of Man,* which defended the ideals of everyone being equal that were behind the French Revolution.

William Pitt (the Elder), 1708–1778, was Prime Minister from 1766 to 1768. He helped to make Britain strong overseas.

William Pitt (the Younger), 1759–1806, was Prime Minister from 1783 to 1801 and from 1804 to 1806. He led Britain through its long war against France (see page 11).

Pitt, the Younger

Sarah Siddons, 1755–1831, was an English actress. She was especially famous for her acting of tragic roles, such as Lady Macbeth.

Adam Smith, 1723–1790, was a Scottish economist who developed the ideas that people's businesses should be allowed to develop without government control and that wealth is created by people doing different, specific jobs.

Thomas Telford, 1757–1834, was a Scottish civil engineer. He built many roads, canals, and bridges, including the suspension bridge across the Menai Straits in Wales.

Richard Trevithick, 1771–1833, developed the world's first steam locomotive (see page 21). This ran on the road. In 1804 he built the first railway locomotive.

J.M.W. Turner, 1775–1851, was one of the greatest of English landscape painters. His pictures show the fantastic effects of light, shadow, and colour.

Robert Walpole, 1676–1745, was the first British Prime Minister. He was in power from 1721 to 1742. He kept his position by rewarding his supporters with well-paid jobs (see page 6).

Mary Wollstonecraft, 1759–1797, was an early feminist writer. Her book, *A Vindication of the Rights of Woman,* argued that women should be allowed to control their own lives.

William IV, 1765–1837, became king after the death of his brother, George IV (see page 40). He reigned for 7 years and was succeeded by Queen Victoria.

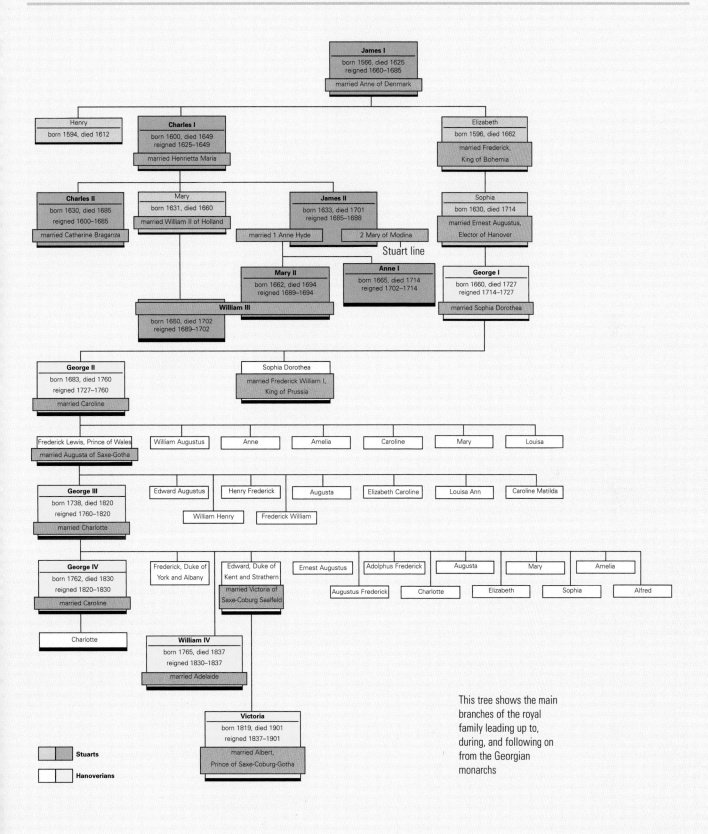

James I
born 1566, died 1625
reigned 1660–1685
married Anne of Denmark

Henry
born 1594, died 1612

Charles I
born 1600, died 1649
reigned 1625–1649
married Henrietta Maria

Elizabeth
born 1596, died 1662
married Frederick,
King of Bohemia

Charles II
born 1630, died 1685
reigned 1600–1685
married Catherine Braganza

Mary
born 1631, died 1660
married William II of Holland

James II
born 1633, died 1701
reigned 1685–1688
married 1 Anne Hyde   2 Mary of Modina

Sophia
born 1630, died 1714
married Ernest Augustus,
Elector of Hanover

Stuart line

Mary II
born 1662, died 1694
reigned 1689–1694

Anne I
born 1665, died 1714
reigned 1702–1714

George I
born 1660, died 1727
reigned 1714–1727
married Sophia Dorothea

William III
born 1650, died 1702
reigned 1689–1702

George II
born 1683, died 1760
reigned 1727–1760
married Caroline

Sophia Dorothea
married Frederick William I,
King of Prussia

Frederick Lewis, Prince of Wales
married Augusta of Saxe-Gotha

William Augustus   Anne   Amelia   Caroline   Mary   Louisa

George III
born 1738, died 1820
reigned 1760–1820
married Charlotte

Edward Augustus   Henry Frederick   Augusta   Elizabeth Caroline   Louisa Ann   Caroline Matilda

William Henry   Frederick William

George IV
born 1762, died 1830
reigned 1820–1830
married Caroline

Frederick, Duke of York and Albany

Edward, Duke of Kent and Strathern
married Victoria of Saxe-Coburg Saalfeld

Ernest Augustus   Adolphus Frederick   Augusta   Mary   Amelia

Augustus Frederick   Charlotte   Elizabeth   Sophia   Alfred

Charlotte

William IV
born 1765, died 1837
reigned 1830–1837
married Adelaide

Victoria
born 1819, died 1901
reigned 1837–1901
married Albert,
Prince of Saxe-Coburg-Gotha

Stuarts

Hanoverians

This tree shows the main branches of the royal family leading up to, during, and following on from the Georgian monarchs

GLOSSARY

allied working or fighting together

Catholics people who are members of the Christian Roman Catholic church led by the Pope in Rome

colony land in one country that is ruled by another country

common land land that is owned and can be used by everyone in a village or community

cotton gin machine that straightens raw cotton fibres so they can be spun

drover someone who drives cattle or other livestock over long distances to be sold

estate property consisting of a large area of land usually with a big house on it

exile being sent away from the country you chose to live in

export sell goods to another country

government people who run the country; the monarch, his Council of ministers, Parliament and local officials, such as magistrates

import bring in goods from another country

iron foundry place where metal is cast, or shaped, by heating, rolling, or hammering

ivory hard material that forms the tusks of elephants and some other animals. It can be carved into beautiful shapes.

magistrate person who acts like a judge to try accused criminals, but in a local court and without a jury. Magistrates deal mostly with minor crimes.

militia type of army made up of part-time soldiers raised from local people. The militia was only called out in an emergency.

musket gun with a smooth barrel that fires small lead balls called shot

mutiny uprising against the people in command. It is usually used to describe rebellions in the army and navy.

navigator person who guides a ship at sea, using charts and instruments such as a compass and a chronometer

parish constable early kind of policeman, appointed to keep law and order by a local parish

press gang group of seamen who press (force) ordinary men to become sailors when there are not enough crew to sail their ship

Protestant member of one of the Christian churches which split from the Catholic Church in the 16th century.

rifle gun with a grooved barrel that is more accurate than a musket

rigging ropes and tackle used to control the sails of a sailing ship

scurvy disease caused by too little Vitamin C in the diet. It causes swellings and sore gums, and is cured by eating fresh fruit and vegetables.

shuttle wooden container that carries the weft (horizontal thread) back and forth between the warp (vertical threads) on a weaving loom

slaves people who are owned by others, for whom they must work without pay

smallpox infectious disease that killed many people in the Georgian Age. It causes a rash of pimples on the face.

spindle rod holding the bobbin on to which yarn or thread is wound

squatter someone who settles on land without having any legal claim to it

tallow oil or candle made from animal fats

Tory one of the main parties in Parliament, which was to become the Conservative Party. Most Tories opposed reform and supported expansion of the empire.

trade union organization of workers set up to negotiate with employers over conditions of pay, hours of work and unemployment benefits

transport punish convicted criminals by sending them to colonies abroad, such as Australia

United Kingdom combination of England, Scotland, Wales (together known as Great Britain) and Northern Ireland. Its flag is the Union Jack.

vaccinate put a substance into somebody's body to protect them from disease

Whig political party in Parliament which opposed the power of the monarch. It became better known as the Liberal party after the 1830s.

workhouse public place in which the poor were fed and housed in return for doing some work

yarn continuous strand made of fibres twisted together. Yarn is used in knitting, sewing or weaving cloth.

Find out more

Books

Admiral Nelson: The Sailor Who Dared All to Win, Sam Llewellyn (Short Books, 2004)

Famous Lives: Captain Cook, Rebecca Levene (Usborne, 2005)

Life in Britain: Britain in the Industrial Revolution, Fiona MacDonald (Franklin Watts, 2003)

Events and Outcomes: The Slave Trade, Tom Monaghan (Evans, 2002)

Witness to History: Industrial Revolution, Stewart Ross (Heinemann Library, 2003)

Websites

www.bbc.co.uk/history

Among other topics, this website covers the kings and queens of the Georgian era.

www.britainexpress.com/History/Georgian_index.htm

An exploration of life and culture in Georgian Britain.

www.britishempire.co.uk

Find out about the early history of the British Empire.

www.georgianindex.net

This website covers all aspects of Georgian style and social life.

www.nmm.ac.uk

The website of the National Maritime Museum, London.

Places to visit

Here are some museums and sites of Georgian interest to visit. Your local Tourist Office will be able to tell you about other places in your area.

Bingley "Five-Rise", Yorkshire   A staircase of five locks on the Leeds and Liverpool Canal.

Chatsworth House, Derbyshire   Magnificent stately home and grounds.

Highland Folk Museum, Kingussie, Scotland   Copies of 18th-century Highland houses.

HMS *Victory*, Portsmouth, Hampshire   Nelson's flagship, restored to its original condition.

Ironbridge Gorge Museum, Shropshire   Many exhibits from the industrial age, including the famous bridge.

North of England Open Air Museum, Beamish, County Durham   Reconstructions of houses and rooms, and exhibits from the industrial revolution.

Royal Crescent, Bath   Curved row of houses designed by John Wood. Number 1 has been restored to its Georgian condition.

Royal Pavilion, Brighton   A fantastic building, designed for the Prince Regent, in a mixture of Indian, Gothic, and Chinese styles.

Stourhead, Wiltshire   Huge landscaped garden, with lakes, temples, and follies.

Welsh Folk Museum, Cardiff   Reconstructions of many old buildings, including a farmworker's cottage and a watermill.

INDEX